William Savage

The Birth-Place, Home, Churches, and Other Places

William Savage

The Birth-Place, Home, Churches, and Other Places

ISBN/EAN: 9783337002664

Printed in Europe, USA, Canada, Australia, Japan

Cover: Foto ©ninafisch / pixelio.de

More available books at **www.hansebooks.com**

THE BIRTH-PLACE, HOME, CHURCHES,

AND OTHER PLACES CONNECTED WITH THE

AUTHOR OF "THE CHRISTIAN YEAR."

THE
BIRTH-PLACE, HOME, CHURCHES,

AND OTHER PLACES

CONNECTED WITH THE

AUTHOR OF "THE CHRISTIAN YEAR,"

Illustrated in Thirty-two Photographs

BY W. SAVAGE;

WITH NOTES

THE REV. J. F. MOOR, JUN., M.A.,
INCUMBENT OF AMPFIELD.

Winchester:
WILLIAM SAVAGE.

London, (377, Strand):
JAMES PARKER AND CO.
1866.

TO

SIR WILLIAM HEATHCOTE,
OF HURSLEY PARK, BART.,
M.P. FOR THE UNIVERSITY OF OXFORD,

AND TO

LADY HEATHCOTE,

This Volume

IS RESPECTFULLY DEDICATED.

CONTENTS.

	PAGE
INTRODUCTION	11
POEM IN MEMORY OF THE REV. JOHN KEBLE	15
MEMOIR OF THE REV. JOHN KEBLE	17
APPENDIX, WITH SUMMARY OF EVENTS	31
MONODY ON THE DEATH OF THE LATE REV. JOHN KEBLE	35
FAIRFORD, THE POET'S BIRTH-PLACE	41
OXFORD	57
EAST LEACH	65
BURTHORPE	69
SOUTHROP	73
COLN ST. ALDWYN'S	81
HURSLEY,—OF WHICH THE POET WAS VICAR	91
OTTERBOURNE,—OF WHICH HE WAS RECTOR	113
AMPFIELD,—OF WHICH HE WAS PATRON	129
PITT,—HIS OUTLYING CHAPELRY	145
BOURNEMOUTH,—WHERE HE DIED	149
THE GRAVES OF MR. AND MRS. KEBLE	153

LIST OF PHOTOGRAPHS.

NO.		PAGE
1.	PORTRAIT . . .	13
2.	REV. J. KEBLE'S BIRTH-PLACE . .	37
3.	,, ,, ,, ,, ,, FROM THE ROAD .	39
4.	,, ,, ,, ,, ,, WITH YEW-TREE .	43
5.	FAIRFORD CHURCH .	47
6.	,, ,, . .	51
7.	CORPUS CHRISTI COLLEGE, OXFORD .	55
8.	ORIEL COLLEGE, OXFORD	59
9.	EAST LEACH CHURCH	63
10.	BURTHORPE CHURCH .	67
11.	SOUTHROP CHURCH .	71
12.	SOUTHROP PARSONAGE . .	75
13.	COLN ST. ALDWYN'S CHURCH, EAST .	79
14.	,, ,, ,, ,, SOUTH	83
15.	HURSLEY CHURCH .	87
16.	,, ,, INTERIOR . .	89
17.	HURSLEY VICARAGE AND CHURCH PORCH	93
18.	HURSLEY CHURCH SPIRE . .	97
19.	,, ,, ,, FROM THE PARK .	101
20.	HURSLEY VICARAGE .	105

c

NO.		PAGE
21.	Hursley Vicarage, South .	107
22.	Otterbourne Church, East	111
23.	,, ,, South	115
24.	Interior of Otterbourne Church	119
25.	Otterbourne Parsonage	123
26.	Ampfield Church . .	127
27.	Interior of Ampfield Church	131
28.	Fountain at Ampfield Church	135
29.	Ampfield Parsonage	139
30.	Pitt Chapel	143
31.	Brookside, Bournemouth . .	147
32.	The Graves of Mr. and Mrs. Keble	151

INTRODUCTION.

THE following brief Notes are not intended in the slightest degree to supply the place of a Life of the Author of "The Christian Year;" but it is felt that *everything* connected with such a saintly man as Mr. KEBLE must needs be of deep interest to all who are looking forward with hope to that rest into which he has entered; and it is thought that the Photographs will not only be looked at with real interest as faithful representations of the places connected with the much-loved name of KEBLE, but will also help the reader of any life of the great Christian poet to represent more clearly to his mind the events recorded about him.

In the imperfect outline of the life of Mr. KEBLE here presented to the reader, much has been taken from letters in "The Guardian" newspaper by an old and well-known friend of the Poet. Some of the events mentioned are as yet known to hardly any one else but the author of these fragmentary notes, whose apology for undertaking this work at the request of the Artist whose Photographs he treats about, is that he has intimately known and reverently loved for many years the holy man of whom, with much diffidence and with deep veneration, he ventures to speak, and that it has been his high privilege to have been placed by him in various offices of trust.

INTRODUCTION.

The writer of these notes presents his best thanks to the many kind friends who have in various ways helped him in making them; amongst whom he ventures to name Sir William and Lady Heathcote, the Rev. the Provost of Oriel College, Oxford, the Rev. Alfred Kent, M.A., Vicar of Coln St. Aldwyn, and the Rev. J. W. Richards, M.A., late Curate of Hursley, as well as the members of Mr. KEBLE'S own family.

Some of the information here given has been derived from "Memoranda of the Parish of Hursley," by the Rev. John Marsh, and many of the facts stated have been verified by reference to parish registers, college papers, and other documents; still, if there should be any inaccuracies (which it is difficult to avoid in a work of this kind), it is hoped that they will be pardoned by the indulgent reader.

John Keble

IN MEMORY

OF THE

REV. JOHN KEBLE.

Printed by permission of the Author.

WHAT time the Angels blest and fair,
    On embassies of love,
Descended from "the lucid stair*,"
    Leaving their songs above;

What time to this sad lower earth
    They stoop'd in human frame—
Sure earnests of that wondrous Birth
    When God Incarnate came;—

It chanc'd one of this Choral band—
    As fancy loves to tell—
To drop unweeting from his hand
    The Lyre he struck so well.

Full many an age preserv'd from harm,
    Conceal'd on earth it lay:
Time could not mar its deathless charm,
    Its power could ne'er decay.

* Hymn for the Eighth Sunday after Trinity.

A Pilgrim meek, of downcast eye,
  "Commercing" with the ground,
Saw it in his humility:
  The Lyre of Heaven was found!

He seiz'd it glad; he tun'd each chord,
  True melodies to give:
His song was "ever of the Lord,"
  And so shall ever live.

But clos'd is now his "Christian Year,"
  Come his Eternal Day:
Peace to our Pilgrim Poet dear,
  And thanks to God alway.
J. F.

THE REV. JOHN KEBLE.

"Non immerito vocaris Johannes id est cui donatum est .... tibi donatum est abdita penetrare mysteria."—*Orig. Hom. II. in diversos.*

THE Author of "The Christian Year" was born at Fairford, in Gloucestershire, on St. Mark's Day, 1792. He was educated by his father (the Rev. JOHN KEBLE, Vicar of Coln St. Aldwyn's), until December, 1806, when (though at that time considerably under fifteen years old), he obtained by competition a scholarship at Corpus Christi College, Oxford, proving by his success the excellent training which his father had given him.

In the Easter Term Examination in 1810, when just eighteen years of age, he obtained a double first-class, a distinction which had been obtained by only one man before that time, namely, the late Sir Robert Peel, by only one other at the same time, and (it is believed) by no one else at any time *at so early an age.*

In the year after this he obtained a fellowship at Oriel College, which was at that time one of the highest distinctions of the University. The distinguished names of Copleston (soon after Provost), Davison (who wrote the standard book on Prophecy), and Whately (afterwards Archbishop of Dublin), were among the electors.

In the following year (1812) Mr. KEBLE obtained the Chancellor's Prize for the English Essay, "On Translation from Dead Languages;" also the Chancellor's Prize for the Latin Essay on the following subject, "Xenophontis res bellicas, quibus ipse interfuit, narrantis, cum Cæsare comparatio."

In Michaelmas Term, 1818, he was appointed College Tutor—an office which he held for about five years. He was deeply beloved by his pupils (amongst whom are some of the most distinguished men of the present day), who on his retiring from that office, presented him with some magnificent and massive plate, bearing the expressive inscription JOHANNI KEBLE DISCIPULORUM ORIELENSIUM PIETAS, MDCCCXXIII.

He was one of the Public Examiners from Michaelmas Term, 1814, for two years, and again from Michaelmas, 1821, to 1823. On Trinity Sunday, 1815, he was ordained Deacon, with his fellowship as his title, and Priest in the following year. His earliest parochial work, which began immediately upon his ordination, consisted chiefly in officiating in the churches of East Leach and Burthorpe, of which he held the curacies for some time. He used to reside at Fairford with his father in vacation time, and, after his appointment to the tutorship at Oriel, during Term time he rode from Oxford every other Saturday to spend Sundays at home, and perform the duty at his curacies: his brother, the Rev. THOMAS KEBLE, having been at the same time appointed Tutor at Corpus Christi College, of which he was Fellow, used to take the duty in the same way on the alternate Sundays; their father undertook the parochial visiting and occasional week-day services in these little parishes for his son during the time of his being in Oxford.

Mr. KEBLE'S taste for poetry was manifested at an early age. As early as the year 1808, he wrote a poem on Mahomet. In the year 1819 he wrote some of the hymns which form part of "The Christian Year;" but the natural and excessive humility of his disposition, which shewed itself throughout his life in a manner almost incredible to those who had not the honour and exceeding great privilege of knowing him, made him shrink from the publication of that great work until he was at last constrained to give way to the urgent advice of his friends; so that in 1827 appeared the first edition of that book which is known, studied, and loved wherever the English language is spoken, and which stands alone in having reached ninety-two English editions (besides those published in America), in the lifetime of its Author; several of the editions consisting of three thousand, and the ninetieth of five thousand copies.

In 1828 Mr. KEBLE was talked of for election to the headship of Oriel, then vacant by the death of Dr. Copleston, when the present Provost (Dr. Edward Hawkins) was elected. In 1831 Mr. KEBLE was elected to the Professorship of Poetry at Oxford, which office he held for two periods of five years, according to the usual custom of that office.

After retiring from the duties of tuition at Oxford, Mr. KEBLE held the curacy of Southrop, living in the vicarage-house there, and taking pupils, from whom he received no remuneration beyond a contribution towards his house-keeping expenses. Amongst his pupils there were the late Rev. Isaac Williams, and the late Archdeacon Wilberforce. He remained there until the latter part of 1825, when he obtained the curacy of Hursley under Archdeacon Heathcote. In October, 1826, he resigned the curacy of Hursley, and went to live with his father, acting as his curate at Coln

St. Aldwyn's, until January, 1835, when death called away his venerable parent; and at the end of the same year Mr. KEBLE was presented to the living of Hursley (then vacant by the resignation of the Rev. G. W. Heathcote, the present Rector of Ash) by his friend and former college pupil, Sir William Heathcote, Bart.

In the year 1831, when Mr. KEBLE was living with his father at Fairford, the present Lord Bishop of Exeter offered to him the valuable living of Paignton, in Devonshire, considering him even then to be "the most eminently good man in the Church," as his Lordship has kindly informed the writer of these lines; adding that "the conscientious scruple of the patron who had purchased that presentation, and who felt doubtful of the propriety of his acquiring Church patronage by such purchase," made him feel it his "duty to use the utmost caution in selecting a person to fill it." His Lordship says "Mr. KEBLE declined it, though he was at the time wholly without preferment, because his aged father was then alive, whom his filial piety would not allow him to quit, and to whom he assiduously devoted his attentions."

On the 10th of October, 1835, Mr. KEBLE was joined in marriage, in the parish church of Bisley (of which his brother, the Rev. THOMAS KEBLE, B.D., had been Vicar for several years), to Miss Charlotte Clarke, the younger daughter of a deceased clergyman, who had been Vicar of Meysey-Hampton, near Fairford, and sister to Mrs. THOMAS KEBLE.

From the time of his induction to the living of Hursley with Otterbourne, up to the day of his death, we have in Mr. KEBLE a model which all country pastors would do well to set before themselves for imitation. His fame was by this time spread throughout the whole English Church;

he had begun that great movement which (though often evil spoken of by men of opposite views) has gradually and unmistakably raised the tone of religious feeling amongst members of the Church in this country. Still this great man, though gifted with extraordinary powers of mind, was content to live a very retired life in an exceedingly small country vicarage, and to condescend to simplify his teaching to suit the capacity of the poor and most unlearned.

In 1846 Mr. KEBLE published the first edition of the *Lyra Innocentium*, the profits of which helped towards the restoration of the parish church of Hursley, which he had set his mind upon accomplishing almost entirely at his own expense. But in order to procure sufficient means for the completion of that work, he for a time entrusted the copyright of " The Christian Year" to his old and valued friend, the Right Hon. Sir J. T. Coleridge, by whose able advice and assistance a large sum of ready money was realized. And thus was built, chiefly out of the profits of that one book of Christian poetry, one of the most beautiful churches in the land.

The same great mind which had given to the world " The Christian Year" was continually active in the cause of the Divine Master, to whom were devoted the firstfruits of the great talents which were profusely bestowed upon it.

Amongst the poetical writings of Mr. KEBLE is included an edition of the Psalms in English Verse, which expresses the force of the original much more than any other metrical translation, whilst the rendering of some of the Psalms is excessively beautiful and poetic. There are also many poems in the *Lyra Apostolica* from the pen of the same author.

Of his prose works there are many which will without doubt be handed down to posterity, and bear good fruit in future ages. Amongst these must be named his books on "Eucharistic Adoration" and "Considerations on the Doctrine of the Most Holy Eucharist," both which have doubtless done much to create in pious communicants increased reverence at the celebration of the Holy Communion, about which he was himself always especially careful, and which he was most anxious to impress by every means in his power upon all those who were at any time under his instruction. These books are strongly recommended to all persons who wish to know and understand clearly the doctrine of the Church of England with regard to the presence of Christ in the Lord's Supper.

There is also a volume of "Sermons Academical and Occasional," which contains a preface well calculated to afford guidance and comfort to any who may be in doubt and difficulty regarding the state and prospects of the Church of England.

Mr. KEBLE'S edition of Hooker, in three volumes 8vo., will always be regarded as the standard edition of the works of that great English divine; and his "Selections from the Fifth Book of Hooker" will be even more extensively useful as being within reach of all persons.

The two volumes of *Prelectiones Academicæ* will afford thought and study for the more learned, while the minds of all may be refreshed by many of those single sermons, letters, addresses, and pamphlets which were so well fitted for the several occasions which called them forth.

A little book of private devotion, written by Mr. KEBLE in 1864, called "A Litany of our Lord's Warnings," shews how deeply he felt the heresy of a denial of eternal punishment. The preface to it may be of great use to the devout reader.

For many of the later years of his life Mr. KEBLE was engaged in the Life of Bishop Wilson, and in that work (forming two volumes of the Library of Anglo-Catholic Theology) he has carefully collected nearly all that could be said in connexion with the name of that great and good man, who was in many respects so much like Mr. KEBLE himself, though living in such different times and placed under such different circumstances.

While Mr. KEBLE was giving to the world these noble fruits of his clear and talented mind, he was always actively engaged in his own parish work at home.

In connexion with his friend and patron Sir William Heathcote (who was always ready, with able advice and liberal donations, to carry on any good work), and other friends, not only was the parish church of Hursley rebuilt, but also (several years previously) that of Otterbourne. A new church was built at Ampfield, and many years afterwards a school chapel erected at Pitt. Besides this, a parsonage-house was built at Otterbourne; and at Hursley and Ampfield houses built for other purposes were given up to the use of the incumbents. Commodious school-rooms were also provided in all three places.

These works of themselves demanded much thought and money, even though the aid of the principal landowners and others was liberally bestowed.

While all these various projects for the good of those under his charge were being performed, the Church's rule for daily prayer, as expressed in the Prayer-book, was vigorously enforced, together with (at least for many years) a weekly celebration of the Holy Communion at Hursley, and a strict observance, as ordered by the Church, of all fasts and festivals.

The same devout mind which had done so much to restore the Church of England to the faith and zeal of former days, was ever active for good in the parish of Hursley. The sick were tended with loving care; the poor were helped in soul and body; the ignorant and ungodly were diligently sought after, warned, and instructed. Clubs and societies were formed for the good of the labouring classes; children were carefully and lovingly trained for God's service.

But besides all this work upon the hands of the Vicar of Hursley, he had a very large correspondence. Persons in difficulty and anxiety found in him so able and kind an adviser, that his counsel was largely sought after, not only in England, Scotland, and Ireland, but also in many of the colonies. The gentle and kind manner in which he gave advice was a great characteristic in that good man. He could enter into the feelings of those who applied to him in a way that very few could ever do. While he carefully shrunk away from the curious gaze of those who merely wanted to see the "Author of the Christian Year," he would never draw back from any one who honestly wished to unfold his heart with real desire for pastoral guidance.

One whose honoured name has already been mentioned in connexion with Mr. KEBLE, and who knew him as a close and dear friend for more than half a century, has publicly testified of him in these words: "Looking back through an intimacy unbroken, unchilled for more than fifty-five years, he seems to me now to have been at once the simplest, humblest, and most loving-hearted man, and withal the holiest and most zealous Christian, I have ever known."

There was something in the manner in which Mr. KEBLE imparted religious instruction, which impressed that instruction upon the hearts of those whom he taught. There was a simplicity, earnestness, and reality in his mode of teaching, which made impression upon even the thoughtless and the careless, almost against their own will. Words spoken by him seemed to have a living force with those to whom he spoke them, and that living force continues with many whom he prepared for Confirmation and first Communion, and not only will continue to the end of their lives, but will doubtless bear fruit in future ages, and in generations yet unborn.

He spared no pains to reclaim those who went astray, and to guide those who needed guidance. In many a dark winter's night, after he had passed the usual span of man's life, he would walk alone, with a lantern in his hand, to some distant part of the widely-scattered parish of Hursley to prepare a few of his flock for Confirmation or Communion. He would have one or two at a time for instruction, that he might teach them more impressively than he could with many together, and he would never grudge hours spent in repeating the same things over and over again to those who were dull and inapt in learning.

If friends were staying with him whose society he wished to enjoy, still he cheerfully left them that he might attend to the poor lads who came to him for instruction. Yet while he was doing all this (his whole soul, mind, and body being given up to his Master's cause) his humility was such, that he would speak of his own parish work almost as if it were an utter failure, and would be beyond measure glad to hear of more showy signs of pastoral activity and success elsewhere.

The writer of these few lines has often heard Mr. KEBLE deeply lamenting his own imaginary want of ability as a parish priest, and that in a spirit of the truest humility. Humility was indeed personified in him.

In the latter part of Mr. KEBLE'S life he had many changes amongst his curates at Hursley. Frequent absence from home, chiefly on account of Mrs. KEBLE'S health, made it needful for Mr. KEBLE to keep two curates for the services at Hursley and Pitt. There was about him such a peculiar loveliness of disposition as endeared him to all who had to serve under him, though it were but for a short time. He could speak reproof when needed, but it was loving reproof, and he would always make every imaginable allowance for the mistakes, faults, or omissions of duty of those about him. But in truth no words can worthily describe the real saintliness of the character of the author of "The Christian Year." Those who knew him loved him, and could not help loving him, and those most intimate with him now know that they have lost in him their best friend on earth.

In the latter part of the year 1864, Mr. KEBLE was very much distressed about the recent judgment of the Privy Council. He was deeply intent upon averting from the Church, as far as might be, the evil effect of that judgment which he so much dreaded. Those who heard him address the Church Congress at Bristol on the 11th of October, 1864, will never forget the deep earnestness with which he spoke about the doctrine of the eternal punishment of the accursed.

These things weighed heavily on his mind; his brain was overtaxed. Without any relaxation of his own parish work he felt it his duty to contend in controversial argument with those who looked upon Church matters in a different light from himself; while at the same time there was the constant strain of deep anxiety for Mrs. KEBLE. All this was too much for him. In the very midst of an important controversy in the evening of St. Andrew's Day, 1864, it pleased God to send upon him a stroke of paralysis—slight indeed, but unmistakable.

From that time, as regards his health and strength, he was an altered man. He was indeed partially raised up, and restored to his friends with much of the freshness of his earlier days, but he was unable to use with safety any great exertion of mind or body. In the following summer he was sufficiently recruited to take some part in the services at church; but he was much from home, both on account of his own impaired health, and that of Mrs. KEBLE.

In the autumn of 1865, he was rendered very anxious by an unusually violent attack of illness sent upon Mrs. KEBLE. On the 11th of October in that year he left Hursley for Bournemouth with Mrs. KEBLE—never to return there again during his life. He was anxious to remain at home over his wedding-day, and it proved to be the last he had to spend on earth.

On the very Sunday before he left home for the last time, besides taking share in the Sunday services in his own parish church, (celebrating the Holy Communion and reading the Lessons,) he walked with the writer of these notes to visit some of his poor people at a distance, and entertained at dinner afterwards some friends who had come unexpectedly to see him. He had about him then his usual simple cheerfulness of manner, though deeply concerned about the feeble state of Mrs. KEBLE, who was confined to her bedroom at that time.

He seemed indeed to fulfil in himself his own words:—

> "Be thou through life a little child;
> By manhood undefiled;
> So shall no Angel grudge thy dreams
> Of fragrance pure and ever brightening beams."
> (*Lyra Innocentium*, p. 191, 1st edit.)

At Bournemouth, Mr. KEBLE for several months fairly enjoyed his health, and seemed lively and active. Mrs. KEBLE continued to fail, and caused him deep anxiety. He looked forward to her death as to a certainty near at hand, and fully trusted in God to support him under the trial which seemed so near him; saying to a friend some such words as these, "If any man ever was prepared for such a trial, surely I have been."

Writing to some friends near his own home early in January, 1866, he spoke of all hope of Mrs. KEBLE'S recovery being gone; but he expressed himself as deeply thankful that the severe attacks of spasmodic asthma from which she had suffered had passed away.

Several friends went to visit him at Bournemouth (amongst others the writer of these notes), and found a most hearty welcome, even in the midst of his deep anxiety. He thanked those who went to see him as if they had conferred a kindness upon him, instead of having received kindness and favour from him in being admitted into his presence, and having heard once more—for the last time—his loving words.

Early in that same January, Mrs. KEBLE seemed at the point of death. It appeared to the medical men and others as if she could not have lived through the first week of the new year. But she was spared a little longer, sometimes reduced to great weakness and then raised up again. It was an anxious time of watching for Mr. KEBLE, and his strength gave way. Scarcely a week of real illness, and he was gone! Gone to rest for ever!

About one o'clock in the morning of the 29th of March, 1866, being Maundy Thursday, his pure spirit was called to quit its frail resting-place. His last words and his last thoughts, even in the semi-conscious moments preceding death, were about the Upper Chamber in Jerusalem, and the Oneness of the Church. Mingled with these thoughts and words were fragments of Latin prayers which he was, up to the last, repeating to himself.

All England seemed stirred at the sad news of the death of the author of "The Christian Year." Multitudes assembled together at his funeral. Two bishops were present; others of the episcopal bench wrote sympathizing letters expressive of their regret at being unable to attend. A great many clergy from London and various other places made a point of following him to the grave. His curates at Hursley, assisted by the surpliced choir, performed the funeral service. Clergy who had worked under his guidance were the pall-bearers. Many a sob was heard—scarcely an eye was tearless. Deep and real sorrow filled the hearts of all who were present at Hursley Church on that never-to-be-forgotten 6th of April, 1866.

Mrs. KEBLE lingered on, (sometimes in great suffering, but with the truest Christian patience, and even with great thankfulness that it had pleased God to take him before her,) until the 11th of May, on which day about noon she fell asleep in Jesus, as he had done six weeks before.

Her funeral, which took place at Hursley on the 18th of May, (exactly six weeks after his,) was by her own wish as much like his as the different circumstances would permit.

The double grave of Mr. and Mrs. KEBLE is near the south-west corner of Hursley churchyard, close to the grave of their sister Elizabeth, and near to the burial-place of the Heathcote family, and to the little path leading from the vicarage to the church, along which the holy man had so often walked on his way to church.

"Calm be his sleep."

APPENDIX.

HE following notices of the KEBLE family, and short summary of events connected with the author of "The Christian Year," may be considered interesting.

The family of KEEBLE, KEBLA, KEBLE, or KIBBLE, seem to have had connexion with the county of Gloucester for many years.

There was one Sir HENRY KEEBLE, who was Lord Mayor of London in 1510, in the reign of Henry VIII. His descendant, RICHARD KEEBLE, purchased the manor of East Leach Turville. This manor is said to have continued for "six generations in the name of KEEBLE," all of which retained the same Christian name of Richard, as it is stated in Sir R. Atkyns's "Ancient and Present State of Gloucestershire," written in 1711, at which time there was still a RICHARD KEEBLE lord of that manor.

The monuments which are mentioned in the accompanying notes, shew that the family have continued to have connexion with that neighbourhood ever since.

The Rev. JOHN KEBLE the elder made his earliest entry in the marriage register of the parish of Coln St. Aldwin in 1782, and retained the benefice until his death on the 24th of January, 1835. The clear and legible handwriting of the two JOHN KEBLES was so much alike that it requires great care to distinguish them one from another in the registers.

The author of "The Christian Year" was born April 25, 1792, admitted Scholar at Corpus Christi College, December 12, 1806, "being as he did assert fourteen years of age on or about the 25th of April last past."

Obtained his double first-class, Easter Term, 1810.

Elected Fellow of Oriel on Friday in Easter-week, 1811; described as being then "of Fairford, in the county of Gloucester."

Obtained the prizes for the English and Latin Essays in 1812.

Admitted full Fellow of Oriel, July 20, 1812.

Took the degree of B.A., July 7, 1810, and of M.A., May 20, 1813.

Was Master of the Schools in 1816.

Tutor at Oriel, Michaelmas, 1818.

Ordained Deacon Trinity Sunday, 1815, and Priest Trinity Sunday, 1816.

Public Examiner, 1814, 1815, 1816, and 1821, 1822, 1823.

Elected Professor of Poetry, 1831.

Wrote "Christian Year," 1819 to 1827.

Held the College Offices of Junior and Senior Treasurer.

First entry in his hand in East Leach parish register of baptisms, October 29, 1815; of burials, April 9, 1816.

First entry in his hand in Burthorpe parish register of baptisms, September 10, 1815; of burials, January 31, 1816.

First entry at Southrop in his own hand, May 4, 1823; last entry, August 8, 1825.

First entry at Coln St. Aldwyn's:—Baptisms, April 28, 1816; burials, January 5, 1816; marriages, December 1, 1816.

APPENDIX.

Last entry at East Leach, July 1, 1828; Burthorpe, August 14, 1825; Colne, June 9, 1835.

At Hursley, first entry of baptism, October 2, 1825, "JOHN KEBLE," Off^g Min^r.

Then follow entries signed "J. KEBLE" to 20th October, 1826.

January 17, 1836, "JOHN KEBLE, Off^g Minister," (in Mr. Christie's writing, he being then Curate).

February 19, 1836, "JOHN KEBLE" in his own hand.

Then on March 20, 1836, "JOHN KEBLE, Vicar."

His last signature in Baptisms was, November 27, 1864, "J. KEBLE," which was his usual signature in registers.

His first entry amongst the burials is on October 2, 1825, "JOHN KEBLE, Off^g Min."

His last as Curate, October 27, 1826, "J. KEBLE."

Then we have one, November 18, 1835, not in his own writing; and December 21, 1835, "J. KEBLE;" and April 1, 1836, "J. KEBLE, Vicar."

His last occasional duty at Hursley was the marriage of Miss Richards (the Curate's eldest daughter) to R. D. Adams, Esq., on the 3rd of October, 1865.

The last time of his preaching was on the 27th of November, 1864, when he preached in his own church in the morning on St. Matt. xxi. 9, and in the afternoon on Isaiah ii. 5.

On the St. Andrew's Day following he catechized in church in the evening service, and on that same night had his seizure.

On the 8th of October, 1865, he celebrated the Holy Communion at 7 A.M., and read the First Lesson at Morning, and the Second at afternoon service. This was the last Sunday of his being at Hursley. On the Wednesday in that week he went with Mrs. KEBLE to Bournemouth, where he died on the 29th of March, 1866, and was buried at Hursley on the 6th of April following.

NOTE.

SINCE these Notes went to the press, the writer has been reminded of the three winters before his last spent by Mr. KEBLE at Penzance, to which place he became much attached, taking share in the services there with much interest, and delighting in the beautiful scenery of the neighbourhood.

Torquay also ought to be mentioned as having been visited by Mr. KEBLE, who spent the former part of one winter there, and afforded occasional help to some of the clergy.

A MONODY

ON THE DEATH OF THE LATE
REV. JOHN KEBLE.

[Inserted by permission of the Author.]

GONE to thy long, last home, thou Christian Bard,
   Whose hallowed harp hath sung The Christian Year!
On earth thy minstrelsy had high reward,
   Higher awaits thee in a higher sphere.
The Saviour's sacrifice, which thou didst sing
   With a most holy praise upon this earth,
Now to thy spirit doth redemption bring,
   Freed from the sin-stains of man's mortal birth;
Sweeping thy golden harp before the Throne,
Where Angels and Archangels hear and know its tone.

Oh! what a glorious, what a heavenly sight,
   When man's immortal soul has burst the clay,
And borne on angel-wings to realms of light,
   First sees the dawn of an eternal day:
First sees, with eyes freed from all earthly scales,
   First feels with Faith, where doubt no more is found,
The everlasting glory that prevails,
   Amidst the hosts of Heaven, all marshalled round;
While seated on the right hand of God's throne
The blessed Saviour there doth His redeemèd own.

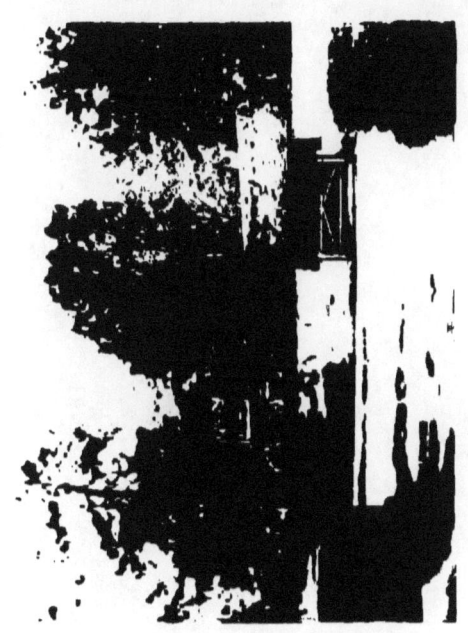

FAIRFORD.

Nos. 2 and 3.

THE house at Fairford, in which Mr. KEBLE was born, was left to him by his father, and has been bequeathed by him to the Rev. THOMAS KEBLE, junior, the only son of his only brother. It is a plain stone building near the road, with a stone wall in front of it, and it forms part of a leasehold property which has been in possession of the family for nearly one hundred years.

Near the house are many large elms, which may have afforded much matter for poetical thought to the great author, such as he expressed in the hymn for the Twenty-third Sunday after Trinity, in the words :—

"Yet wait awhile, and see the calm leaves float
    Each to his rest beneath their parent shade.

How like decaying life they seem to glide!
    And yet no second spring have they in store,
But where they fall, forgotten to abide
    Is all their portion, and they ask no more.

Soon o'er their heads blithe April airs shall sing,
    A thousand wild-flowers round them shall unfold,
The green buds glisten in the dews of Spring,
    And all be vernal rapture as of old.

Unconscious they in waste oblivion lie,
    In all the world of busy life around
No thought of them; in all the bounteous sky
    No drop, for them, of kindly influence found."

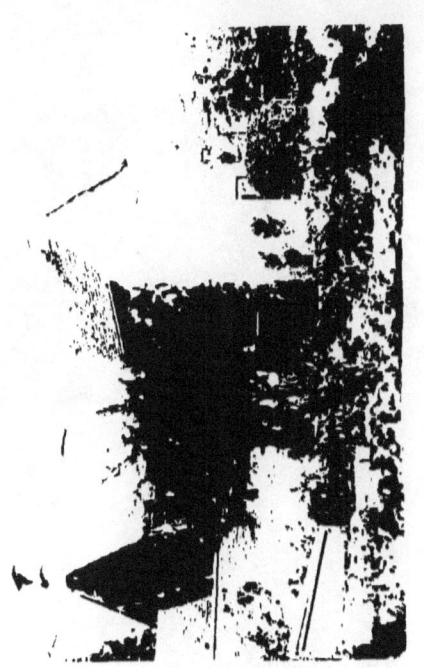

FAIRFORD.

No. 4.

BENEATH the overshadowing boughs of the elm-trees is a gravel path surrounding an orchard and small paddock, from which it is fenced off by posts and chains. This path is said to have formed a favourite walk for the Poet, who thus refreshed himself from his studies under the cool shade of the lofty trees.

In his later life he used to speak of this walk as having afforded him much pleasure in his early days, and he compared it with his private walk at Hursley from the vicarage to the boys' schoolroom, under the noble trees which skirt Sir William Heathcote's park.

There is also a yew-tree (which is represented in plate 3) just outside the Poet's study window, under which he is said to have composed many of his beautiful verses.

His father lived and died in this house, having found no difficulty in performing from thence his pastoral duty at Coln St. Aldwyn's, which is only about three miles distant.

FAIRFORD.

No. 5.

FAIRFORD is a small town (of 1,654 inhabitants at the last census) situated amongst the celebrated Coteswold Hills, near the river Coln, about eight miles from Cirencester. It probably derived its name from the beauty of the rich and varied scenery near the banks of the river, which no doubt was suggestive to the Poet of many of his beautiful thoughts.

The present church at Fairford, which is in the Perpendicular style upon a Norman foundation, was begun about the year 1493 by a wealthy merchant named John Tame, and completed by his son, Sir Edmund Tame, Knight. It is adorned with beautiful painted glass windows, supposed by some to have been designed by Albert Durer, but by others to have been the work of Francesco Francia, of Boulogne, a noted man for that kind of work in those days. The great west window contains a wonderful representation of the blessings and the terrors of the Day of Judgment. Our Lord is represented seated on a rainbow, having His feet on the earth, with large brilliant circles around Him, on which are painted countless figures of saints and angels looking towards Him in joyous adoration, mingled with spirits of the departed who have been summoned for judgment. A sword on Christ's left hand, and a sceptre, terminated by a lily, on His right hand, represent Justice and Mercy. Further down in the window is a figure of St. Michael holding the scales to weigh those who are called up for their final sentence. On one side St. Peter is represented with his key, letting the blessed into heaven, and on the other side the devil and his angels are dragging the accursed into hell, and tormenting them in various ways in the midst of the fearful flames of the bottomless pit.

The eastern windows represent the Crucifixion and its attendant circumstances.

The windows of the north aisle are almost entirely representations of Old Testament characters; while those of the south aisle represent characters and events connected with the New Testament.

The clerestory windows on the south represent protectors and saints of the early Church, those on the north side her persecutors.

For a more accurate and detailed account of these windows, the reader is referred to a very interesting paper in the "Monthly Packet" for June, 1866, and to a "History of the Town and Church of Fairford," by the parish clerk, who, as a boy, was servant in the Keble family.

But no one can properly judge of the quaintness and beauty of these windows (of which there are twenty-eight in number) without a careful personal inspection of them.

These windows are said to have been taken from a vessel captured by John Tame when on its voyage to Rome from the Low Countries. There is a tradition that in the troubles during the reign of Charles I., and in the Protectorate, this beautiful glass was saved from destruction by being buried: having been dug up after the Restoration, it was replaced in the church, though in a very mutilated condition.

The early association of the author of "The Christian Year" with the fine church at Fairford, and its beautiful windows, would lead him to admire ecclesiastical decoration, which in his later years he studied with the holy purpose of making it tend to the glory of God, and the promotion of feelings of reverence in Christian worshippers.

FAIRFORD.

No. 6.

THE graves of Mr. KEBLE'S father and mother, and of two of his sisters, are in the churchyard at Fairford, near the path on the south side of the church. In the chancel there is a mural tablet, erected by Mr. KEBLE himself, with the following inscription:—

"Blessed are the dead which die in the Lord."

THESE WORDS ARE HERE DEDICATED IN HUMBLE HOPE
TO THE MEMORY OF MANY FAITHFUL CHRISTIANS OF ONE NAME AND FAMILY,
WHOSE BODIES LIE BURIED, SOME IN THIS CHANCEL,
SOME IN THE ADJOINING CHURCHYARD,
AND ESPECIALLY TO THE MOST REVERED AND PRECIOUS MEMORY
OF THE REV. JOHN KEBLE, M.A.,
SOMETIME FELLOW OF C.C.C., OXFORD,
VICAR FOR FIFTY YEARS OF COLN SAINT ALDWYN'S, NEAR FAIRFORD,
WHO DIED JAN. XXIV., MDCCCXXXV., AGED LXXXIX. YEARS;
OF HIS TWO SISTERS, MARY KEBLE AND ANNE KEBLE,
WHO DIED MARCH XX., MDCCCV. AND JULY XXII., MDCCCIX.,
AGED LXVIII. AND LV. YEARS;
AND OF SARAH HIS WIFE,
DAUGHTER OF THE REV. JOHN MAULE, OF RINGWOOD, HANTS.,
WHO DIED MAY XI., MDCCCXXIII., AGED LXIV. YEARS,
AND OF THEIR TWO DAUGHTERS, SARAH AND MARY ANNE,
WHO DIED JUNE XVI., MDCCCXIV. AND SEPTEMBER XX., MDCCCXXVI.,
AGED EIGHTEEN AND TWENTY-SEVEN YEARS.

"Blessed are the dead which die in the Lord: even so saith the Spirit, for they rest from their labours."

There is also on the floor of the chancel, within the altar-rails on the south side, a lozenge-shaped tablet with the inscription, M. KEBLE, 1744.

OXFORD.

No. 7.

CORPUS CHRISTI COLLEGE was founded in the year 1516 by Richard Fox, Bishop of Winchester, for a President, twenty Fellows, and as many Scholars, "all to be elected from certain specified dioceses and counties." In the election of Scholars a preference was usually given to the younger candidates, and yet, even at the time of Mr. KEBLE'S election, the obtaining a scholarship there was considered a great honour and a mark of much advancement in learning.

Many men who have distinguished themselves in after life began their Oxford career as Scholars of this college. The lecture-rooms in which Mr. KEBLE attended his first college lectures are over the gateway, the large window looking into the quadrangle. This college is pleasantly situated near the Christchurch meadows, towards which some of the rooms look out. The colleges of Christchurch, Oriel, and Merton, are in its immediate vicinity.

Oriel College, though it had not the honour of preparing Mr. KEBLE for his double first-class, has far more claim to be called the college of the author of "The Christian Year" than Corpus has, for his connexion with Oriel was much longer than his connexion with Corpus; in fact, he was connected with Oriel from the age of nineteen until his death.

OXFORD.

No. 8.

ORIEL COLLEGE was founded by Edward II. and Adam de Brome, his almoner, in 1326, for a provost and ten fellows. This number was afterwards increased to eighteen by the liberality of various benefactors, by whom also at different times several scholarships and exhibitions have been founded.

At the time of Mr. KEBLE'S election, and for some years afterwards, a fellowship at Oriel was one of the very highest distinctions which could be gained at Oxford. Amongst the Fellows of Oriel were some of the ablest men of the day. Oriel has always been in high repute, but it was eminently so during the time that Mr. KEBLE, and other men hardly inferior to him in talent, were tutors there. Many most noted names belonging to this college may be found high up in the class-lists of those times; amongst whom may be mentioned the Right Hon. Sir George Grey, Bart.; Sir W. Heathcote, Bart., M.P.; the Right Hon. Sir Charles Wood, Bart.; Bishop Denison; the Right Hon. T. H. S. Sotheron-Estcourt; and the Ven. Archdeacon R. I. Wilberforce.

There is no doubt that the personal influence of Mr. KEBLE as a college tutor has had, and is now having, an inconceivably great effect for good, both in Church and State. Words spoken to a few in his lecture-room at Oriel by the author of "The Christian Year" have borne fruit largely for the good of the Church.

While we look at the venerable buildings of Oriel, stately, massive, of ornamental construction, but not gaudy nor ostentatious, we may well think of that humble but great and good man who was a member of that college close upon fifty-five years. It is not unworthy of note that not only had Mr. KEBLE himself, and his patron Sir William Heathcote, connexion with Oriel College, but that also the two clergymen, whom Mr. KEBLE presented in succession to the incumbency of Ampfield, were of the same college.

# EAST LEACH.

No. 9.

NEAR to the river Leach, which is a tributary of the Thames, and runs into it at Leachlade, are situated the two churches of the small parishes of East Leach and Burthorpe (pronounced *Butherup*), which latter is sometimes called East Leach Martin, the former being distinguished as East Leach Turville, or Tourville. The two churches are very near together, being hardly more than a stone's throw apart, the stream running between them. Mr. KEBLE held the curacies of these two small parishes for nearly eight years immediately following his ordination, as appears from the entries in his hand in the parish registers. During this time he lived with his father at Fairford, except when he was obliged to be in Oxford.

At Michaelmas, 1818, Mr. KEBLE became Tutor at Oriel, and his brother Tutor at Corpus; then in Term time their father undertook the parochial visiting and occasional services in the week in these little parishes, and the brothers took the duty on alternate Sundays, one brother riding over from Oxford one Saturday to spend Sunday at home, and the other brother doing so on the following Saturday.

BURTHORPE.

No. 10.

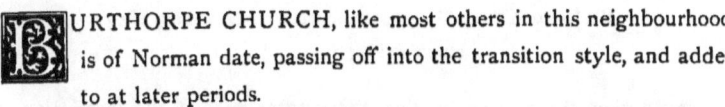URTHORPE CHURCH, like most others in this neighbourhood, is of Norman date, passing off into the transition style, and added to at later periods.

The village to which this church belongs is a mile distant from the church; while East Leach Turville (with its church) is close by.

At the entrance of this latter church is a beautiful carving in stone of Christ blessing little children, with figures of angels at each side.

There are traces of Norman, Early English, and Decorated architecture in Burthorpe church.

The three small lancet windows at the east end are very beautiful and well-proportioned, though at present much spoilt by the hand of some well-meaning plasterer, who has disfigured the bottom part of them.

This church has evidently at one time been much larger, as some arches on the north side mark the place of a former north aisle.

There are monumental stones in the floor commemorating the KEBLE family, to whom the manor of East Leach Tourville belonged for many years. Upon one of the stones, of a dark colour and hard material (apparently marble) is inscribed—

"RICHARD KEBLE, GENEROSUS, NATUS 31 OCTOBER, 1630,
OBIIT 25 JULII, 1701."

On another stone close by this, the greater part of the inscription is illegible because it is partially covered by the floor of a pew, but there is enough to shew that it belongs to the KEBLE family.

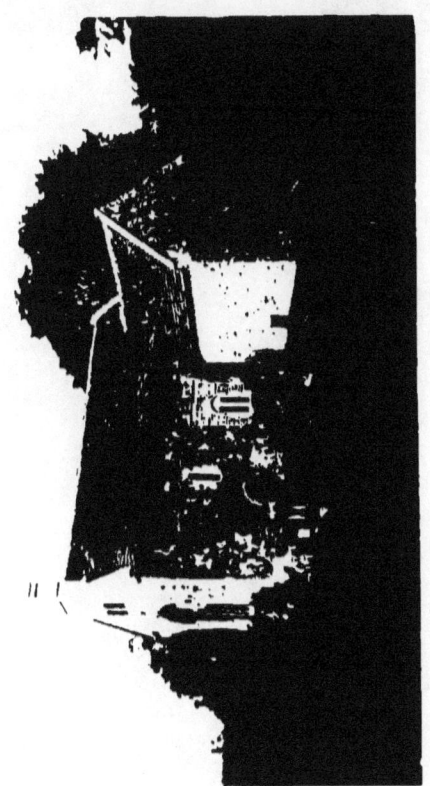

SOUTHROP.

No. 11.

AFTER resigning his tutorship at Oriel, Mr. KEBLE undertook the charge of the parish of Southrop, (usually pronounced *Sutherup*,) another little village near Fairford. Here he lived in the parsonage-house, and was visited by many of his old pupils, whom he assisted in their studies during vacation time, but would receive from them no remuneration, except a contribution towards his house-keeping. Amongst these guests and voluntary pupils of the Poet at Southrop were the distinguished and much-esteemed names of Williams, Wilberforce, Ryder, Heathcote, Prevost, and Hurrell Froude.

The little church at Southrop is of Norman date, with Perpendicular additions. It has a very curious circular font, apparently of late Norman date, which Mr. KEBLE discovered built into an old south doorway of the church, and caused to be removed to its present position at the west end. On this font there is carved a series of figures representing the Christian Virtues, which are trampling under foot and inflicting punishment upon the contrary Vices. This seems meant to teach that by Holy Baptism grace is given a "world of passions to destroy." Around the top of the font there is a band of tracery.

SOUTHROP.

No. 12.

N the wall of the south transept of Southrop Church is a white marble slab, with a centre of black marble bearing the following inscription in gold letters:—

"EDMUND, SON OF THOMAS KEBLE, GENT., DEPARTED THIS LIFE DEC. 30, 1654; JANA, UXOR P: POSUIT DEC. 30, 1656."

The "P:" is supposed to mean *Pia*.

On the south wall of the chancel is a much larger monument, bearing the following inscription :—

"THOMAS KEBLA, SEN., GENT., DECEASED THE 9TH DAY OF AUGUST, ANNO DOMINI 1670; ELIZABETH, UXOR POSUIT."

The arms and crest of the KEBLE family are found close by, having been removed from above the monument. The spelling of the name "Kebla" for KEBLE on this monument is remarkable.

In the churchyard there are several tombstones, on which is inscribed the name KIBBLE, belonging possibly to ancestors of Mr. KEBLE, or descendants of his ancestors.

There are at present several labouring people of the same name residing in the parish.

The vicarage at Southrop is a comfortable little house, though an unpretending building, devoid of architectural beauty, situated near the church, with a spacious and well-planned garden surrounding it. Wadham College, Oxford, possesses the patronage of the living.

COLN ST. ALDWYN'S.

Nos. 13 and 14.

THE Church at Coln (pronounced by the poor people *Cown*) St. Aldwyn (otherwise called Aldwyn's; or, as Mr. KEBLE used to spell it in the register, Aldwin's), of which Mr. KEBLE'S father was vicar for half a century, assisted at the end of his life by Mr. KEBLE himself, is a handsome structure, well restored and kept in excellent repair, standing on the summit of a hill. There is an inscription on a brass plate at the east end, in connexion with two memorial windows, to commemorate the incumbency of Mr. KEBLE'S father, in the following words:—

"✠ TO THE GLORY OF GOD AND THE PIOUS MEMORY OF THE REV. JOHN KEBLE, 50 YEARS VICAR OF THIS CHURCH, OB. 24 JAN., 1835, ✠ THESE TWO EASTERN WINDOWS ARE DEDICATED ✠."

The church is adorned with several painted windows from subjects of both Old and New Testaments.

The parish of Coln St. Aldwyn's had a population of 516 at the last census. The living is in the gift of the Dean and Chapter of Gloucester. At the time of the incumbency of Mr. KEBLE'S father it yielded hardly £50 a-year, the whole of which he spent on the poor of the parish. It is now worth more than double that sum. The village is about three miles from Fairford, and nine from Cirencester. The river Coln, from which Coln St. Aldwyn's is named, flows through the village. On an island in this river there used to be a beautiful clump of willows, which in connexion with the surrounding scene seems to have suggested to the Poet the words,—

> " The May winds gently lift the willow leaves ;
>   Around the rushy point comes weltering slow
> The brimming stream ; alternate sinks and heaves
>   The lily-bud, where small waves ebb and flow.
>   Willow-herb and meadow-sweet !
>   Ye soft gales, that visit there,
>   From your waving censers greet
>   With store of freshest, balmiest air."
>   (*Lyra Innocentium*, p. 182, 1st edit.)

Probably also the same river, and its banks, may have been in the mind of the Poet when in later years he called back the peaceful memories of his early life, and putting them in thought side by side with scenes in Hursley Park, and the extensive woods between Hursley and Ampfield, he said :—

> " Come, take a woodland walk with me
>   And mark the rugged old oak-tree ;
>   How steadily his arm he flings,
>   Where from the bank the fresh rill springs,
>   And points the waters' silent way
>   Down the wild maze of reed and spray.
>   Two furlongs on they glide unseen,
>   Known only by the lovelier green."
>   (*Lyra Innocentium*, p. 205.)

Looking at the little streams of the Coln and the Leach, and then carrying our thoughts to Oxford with its two beautiful rivers, we can imagine the Poet taking a quiet walk in early spring, and expressing his poetic musings in the words:—

> " Lessons sweet of spring returning,
>   Welcome to the thoughtful heart!
> May I call ye sense or learning,
>   Instinct pure, or Heaven-taught art?
> Be your title what it may,
> Sweet the lengthening April day,
> While with you the soul is free,
> Ranging wild o'er hill and lea.
>
> * * * * *
>
> " See the soft green willow springing
>   Where the waters gently pass,
> Every way her free arms flinging
>   O'er the moist and reedy grass.
> Long ere winter blasts are fled,
> See her tipp'd with vernal red,
> And her kindly flower display'd
> Ere her leaf can cast a shade.
>
> " Though the rudest hand assail her,
>   Patiently she droops awhile,
> But when showers and breezes hail her,
>   Wears again her willing smile.
> Thus I learn Contentment's power
> From the slighted willow bower,
> Ready to give thanks and live
> On the least that Heaven may give."

Indeed if any one ever perfectly practised throughout life this lesson of contentment which may be learnt from the willow by the water-side, it was the Poet himself, who has taught it to us not only by those beautiful lines, but still more by his saintly life.

Before we take leave of Coln St. Aldwyn's, with its handsome church and rich scenery, we must notice the substantial stone house, now a comfortable vicarage, but in the Poet's time only a small cottage: here Mr. KEBLE lived occasionally, though his home was at Fairford, only three miles distant. The lower window represented in the accompanying photograph is that of the Poet's study.

Soon after the death of his father, which took place on the 24th of January, 1835, Mr. KEBLE took up his residence entirely in this little cottage, with his only surviving sister. They lived here together until about the month of June in that year. The reluctance with which they then left it is to this day in the memory of some of the older inhabitants of Coln, who as long as they live will continue to revere the name of KEBLE, and to feel deep love for the Christian Poet who laboured amongst them as curate for about nine years.

HURSLEY CHURCH, INTERIOR.

HURSLEY.

Nos. 15—21.

THE parish church of All Saints at Hursley (or, as it was anciently spelt, Hurstleghe, i.e. 'the place in the wood,') seems to have been, (as Mr. KEBLE himself often used to say,) at least, the fourth building upon the same, or very nearly the same, site. Those who remember the church at Hursley twenty or thirty years ago will find little vestige of that building in the present magnificent structure, which cost £6,030. The red brick walls, low tower, and high pews of the old church have been replaced by substantial stone walls, a well-proportioned tower, terminated by a beautiful spire, and remarkably good oak seats, which may well be taken as a model for all church builders who have in view the power of kneeling without inconvenience. Yet Mr. KEBLE was so anxious to preserve all that was worth preserving in the old building, that the proportions of the old and new churches are in the main the same. The old tower remains, only it was in part rebuilt, heightened, and surmounted by its elegant spire, at a cost of £800, at the expense of the liberal Baronet who is the patron of the living. This spire forms a beautiful object, (as represented in the annexed photographs,) from the vicarage garden, from the Walnut avenue in the park, and from various distant places. The most distant view of it is from the high ground on Chilworth Common, near Southampton, from whence the white stonework

shews out clearly in contrast with the dark trees forming the background. In the lower part of the tower may be seen evidences of the work of construction, destruction, and re-construction of former ages; many of the stones with mouldings of earlier date than the tower itself having been worked into the walls, as if on purpose to tell us of former buildings. In the churchyard there are many stately lime-trees, which are supposed to have been planted there by Richard Cromwell, who lived at Hursley Park, and lies buried in the chancel of the church, together with many of his family, as we find recorded on a mural monument which is now inside the south wall of the tower, having been removed to that place from the chancel on the rebuilding of the church. The church consists of a tower, nave, chancel, and two aisles, that on the north side being longer than the other, which irregularity of outline adds greatly to the beauty of the church.

There are doors with porches on the north and south sides, as well as an entrance at the west end of the church, under the tower, and a small door near the end of the south aisle.

Entering the church through the door in the tower, the visitor is struck with the sombre and devotional appearance of the whole building. All seems to speak of peace, and rest, and heaven.

Of this beautiful church well may it be said, in the words of the sacred Poet himself :—

> " The Saints are there—the living dead,
> The mourners glad and strong ;
> The sacred floor their quiet bed,
> Their beams from every window shed,
> Their voice in every song.

HURSLEY CHURCH SPIRE.   No. 18

> "And haply where I kneel, some day,
> From yonder gorgeous pane,
> The glory of some saint will play:
> Not lightly may it pass away,
> But in my heart remain."
>
> *Lyra Innocentium*, p. 265.

All the windows (except those in the roof, which were added a few years ago to give more light in the nave) are filled with painted glass of the richest and most costly description from the celebrated manufactory of Mr. Wailes, and nearly all of them were presented by different persons, Sir William and Lady Heathcote giving one,—the Marchioness of Lothian another. The central west window, which is not a large one, and was the last painted window erected in the church (about the year 1858), represents the final Judgment, according to a very common custom in ancient churches. Our Lord is represented passing sentence on the dead, as in the great west window at Fairford; St. Michael holds the scales; those who are found wanting are placed on the left hand and rejected, while those on the right hand are accepted.

On the north side of the church, here as at Fairford, are represented subjects from the Old Testament. The east window of the north aisle represents the Circumcision of our Lord. The Crucifixion, and some of its attendant events, are depicted in the east window of the church. Special pains were taken with this window by Mr. KEBLE himself, by Mr. Butterfield, who corrected the design, and by Mr. Wailes: the colouring of it is considered to be peculiarly soft and good. All the windows on the south side of the church, including the west window of the south

aisle, contain subjects from the New Testament, or connected with it, so that in looking at the windows in order, going round from the west end of the north aisle to the west end of the south aisle, we are presented with a kind of outline of Bible history, and are well furnished with much matter for profitable thought and holy meditations.

The beautiful carved walnut-wood of the stalls, pulpit, lectern, and altar-rails, are well worthy of notice.

The coronæ and bracket, and standard candlesticks, are very elegant, and well placed for lighting up the whole church.

The font-cover is remarkably handsome; it was presented anonymously about the year 1855, and is a great ornament to the south-west corner of the church.

The angels with shields carved in oak forming the corbels of the roof must also be noticed as being very beautiful, and reminding us of the words on "carved angels" in the *Lyra Innocentium* :—

> "Haply some shield their arms embrace,
> Rich with the Lord's own blazonry;
> The cross of His redeeming grace,
> Or His dead wounds, we there descry.
>   His standard bearers they:
> Learn we to face them on the dread procession day."

The font, lectern, altar-rails, and other fittings of the church, were presents from different persons. The church was consecrated on the 24th of October, 1848, and at the same time a new piece was added to the churchyard, which was further enlarged in the autumn of 1865, by grants of land from the patron and the vicar.

The present vicarage at Hursley, which is situated at the west of the

church between the churchyard and the park, is a picturesque building begun by Sir Thomas Heathcote, the uncle of the present baronet, for a particular object which he had in view, but finished by the present baronet, who allowed it to be used as a residence for the vicar, and afterwards gave it up to the living by a deed bearing date 10th of November, 1842, that it might henceforth become the vicarage instead of the old house, which was considered unfit for the vicar to live in, although it is still attached to the living, as well as the new vicarage.

This new vicarage, though small, is a very pretty house, and is well sheltered by magnificent cedars, elms, and other large trees; in this respect reminding us of the Poet's birth-place.

The vicarage walls, which are chiefly composed of flint and brick with stone dressings, are tastefully adorned with Banksia roses, luxuriant ivy, and Virginian creeper. The grounds around the house were very tastefully laid out by the Poet himself, who also added considerably to the house.

Mr. KEBLE also some years afterwards erected a lych-gate and cottage at the north-east corner of the churchyard, on some ground which he bought and gave up to the living, thinking possibly at the time of his own words:—

> "This is the portal of the dead.
> . . . . .
> This is the holy resting-place
> Where coffins and where mourners wait,
> Till the stoled priest hath time to pace
> His path toward the eastern gate,
> Like one who bears a hidden seal
> Of pardon from a king, where rebels trembling kneel."

OTTERBOURNE.

No. 22.

THE author of "The Christian Year" has often been spoken of as the Vicar of Hursley, but it seems not to have been generally known that he was Rector of Otterbourne, which is a large village on the high road between Winchester and Southampton, about three miles distant from Hursley.

It is recorded that between the years 1296 and 1300, during the incumbency of Hugo de Welewyck, the great tithes of Hursley were alienated by Johannes de Pontissera (or John Points), Bishop of Winchester, and given by him to the college of St. Elizabeth at Winchester.

By this act (which was confirmed by Gulielmus de Edington, or Edyngton, the predecessor of the famous William of Wykeham, in the year 1362) the living of Hursley was reduced to a vicarage.

At the Reformation, the college of St. Elizabeth being dissolved, the great tithes of Hursley were annexed to the cathedral, and became the property of the Dean and Chapter, to whom they still belong, though held under a lease by Sir William Heathcote.

It is somewhat curious, that as a John and a William were spoilers of the church at Hursley in the fourteenth century, so in the nineteenth a John and a William were the great restorers.

In order to make up to the Incumbent of Hursley for the loss of his rectorial tithes, the above-named spoilers (it seems) committed a further, and even more serious alienation, by taking away from Otterbourne its tithes both rectorial and vicarial, and giving them to the Vicar of Hursley, intending by this means to make compensation to him for the loss of his own proper rectorial tithes.

Thus Otterbourne was reduced to a curacy dependent upon Hursley. So that to the present day the tithes of Otterbourne form the most important part of the stipend of the Vicar of Hursley; and yet Otterbourne (if mentioned *at all* in connexion with the author of "The Christian Year") is deprived of the credit of having been his rectory, and of having contributed so largely towards his clerical income.

OTTERBOURNE.

No. 23.

WHEN Mr. KEBLE succeeded to the Rev. G. W. Heathcote as Vicar of Hursley and Rector of Otterbourne, early in the year 1836, he found at the latter place an old church in a somewhat dilapidated condition, and at a considerable distance from the village.

It was soon settled to build a new church near to the village, leaving the old church to be used only as a kind of cemetery chapel whenever it might be required for that purpose.

By the liberal exertions of the principal landowners and others, this plan was soon carried out, and in 1837 the present church was begun to be built, in a most convenient situation, upon a piece of ground presented by Magdalen College, the lords of the manor. Two years later it was consecrated [a]. It cost £3,500, and will hold 428 persons.

The late William C. Yonge, Esq., (father of the author of the "Heir of Redclyffe,") took the matter of church building vigorously in hand, as he did afterwards at Ampfield. To his exertions, and that of his family, the parish of Otterbourne is mainly and deeply indebted for the beauty of its church, which, though it might not satisfy the architectural critic of the present day, is a gem considering the time in which it was built.

[a] The first stone was laid on Tuesday in Whitsun-week, 16th of May, 1837; it was consecrated on the 30th of July, 1839.

OTTERBOURNE.

No. 24.

THE altar-rails in Otterbourne Church consist of finely carved oak, supposed by some to represent the coronation of Richard Cœur de Lion. There are some beautiful painted windows in the church, erected as memorials of members of the Yonge family. The carved work of the pulpit also is much admired. The skilful hand of a lady is discernible in the painting of the Commandments, Creed, and texts around the altar. The churchyard is adorned with choice shrubs, and surrounded by a substantial flint wall, above which, on the roadside, there is an excellent holly hedge, which was raised from the berries of the hollies used to adorn the church on the first Christmas after its consecration.

The boys' school at Otterbourne, which adjoins the churchyard, is an ornamental building adorned with an oriel window, and other relics of the old church; it was built about the same time as the church. There is a girls' school a little lower down the village, which owes its erection to the liberality of Mrs. Bargus, a lady who owned that property in the parish which has been inherited by the Yonges, and who died in 1843.

OTTERBOURNE.

No. 25.

OTTERBOURNE PARSONAGE is at the other end of the village, at some distance from the church. It is an ornamental house, built after a very tasteful design, at the expense of the Rector, costing nearly £1,500, the greater part of which had been saved by Mr. KEBLE during his residence at Oxford, with a view to some such purpose.

AMPFIELD.

No. 26.

ABOUT two miles and a half from Hursley, and four from Otterbourne, by the side of the turnpike-road between Winchester and Romsey, at a distance of a little less than seven miles from Winchester, and a little more than four from Romsey, stands the church of St. Mark at Ampfield. This church, which has 306 sittings, was built at a cost of £3,248, at the sole expense of Sir William Heathcote, who also gave the land for the church and churchyard. The late Joseph White, Esq., of Ampfield House, contributed £500 towards the endowment. The foundation-stone was laid by the third son of the Baronet on St. Matthew's Day, 1838, and it was consecrated on the 21st of April, 1841, and a district parish formed out of the parish of Hursley assigned to it under an act of 58 George III. cap. 45, sect. 21. The incumbency is endowed partly by the interest of an endowment fund paid through Queen Anne's bounty, partly by portions of the rectorial and vicarial tithes of Hursley.

The church is a remarkably good building for the time at which it was erected, when a taste for ecclesiastical architecture was just beginning to be aroused in this country. It is chiefly in the Early English style of architecture; the stonework of the west window, copied from Beverley

Minster, forming an excellent specimen of that beautiful style, and the east window being copied from one in Lincoln Cathedral.

The building consists of a nave, chancel, and small aisle, with a gallery on the north side, used by the boys of the Sunday-school, and a porch with vestry over it on the south side. The walls are remarkably thick and substantial, especially the west wall, which supports a bell-turret, designed from one at the church of Leigh Delamere in Wiltshire. This little turret terminates in a slender spire, with a metal cross on the top of it.

INTERIOR OF AMPFIELD CHURCH.

AMPFIELD.

No. 27.

ABOUT the year 1855, a painted east window, which cost £100, was presented to Ampfield Church by the Rev. R. F. Wilson, the first incumbent, and about the same time, Sir William and Lady Heathcote and Mrs. R. F. Wilson joined together to present, at a still greater cost, a magnificent west window.

The east window, which is in four lights, is descriptive of four of the chief events of our Lord's humiliation, with the inscription " He humbled Himself and became obedient unto death, even the death of the cross," contrasted with four acts of His exaltation, with the inscription "Wherefore God also hath highly exalted Him, and given Him a name which is above every name."

The west window, which has three large lights, contains sixteen medallions descriptive of the last Judgment, again reminding us of the west windows at Fairford. Our Lord in Judgment, seated on a rainbow, is represented in the upper part of the middle light with the Holy Spirit above Him in the form of a dove. In the upper medallion of each sidelight the Holy Apostles are represented. The four lower medallions on the south side represent acts of faith, and the state of the blessed; the corresponding medallions on the north side represent evil actions, and the damnation of the accursed.

The visitor will be particularly delighted with the churchyard at Ampfield. Here indeed is 'God's acre'—a peaceful place of repose for the dead—almost surrounded with wood, and abounding with evergreens of the choicest varieties, which flourish in great luxuriance, while the rhododendrons grow to great size, and adorn the place with their beautiful flowers in the months of May and June.

From the church door may be seen, towards the south, the outline of the Isle of Wight and part of the New Forest.

FOUNTAIN AT AMPFIELD CHURCH. No. 28.

AMPFIELD.

No. 28.

CLOSE to the lower entrance of Ampfield Churchyard there is a drinking-fountain surmounted by a cross, erected in 1845 by Sir William and Lady Heathcote and a Miss Trench (now Mrs. R. F. Wilson), in remembrance of one seen by them during a tour in the Tyrol.

The inscription inviting the thirsty traveller to drink reminds him of the thirst which we *should* have for heavenly things :—

"While cooling waters here ye drink
Rest not your thoughts below;
Look to the sacred sign, and think
Whence living waters flow;
Then fearlessly advance by night or day—
The holy Cross stands guardian of your way."

The idea of this last line is borrowed from the poem in the *Lyra Innocentium* on "Lifting up to the Cross."

Having refreshed himself, he looks up and sees towering over the dark green hollies above him the little church spire, like a "silent finger" pointing up to heaven, in which there is no more hunger nor thirst for ever.

On the trough into which the water runs is the following inscription in German :—

W.H. M.T. S.H.
Zur Erinnerung an
Heiliges Wasser
Tyrol,
1845.

AMPFIELD.
No. 29.

A LITTLE further on the road towards Romsey, on the right-hand side, is situated Ampfield Parsonage—a small house which was presented to the incumbency by Sir William Heathcote, by a deed bearing date 25th of March, 1844. It is delightfully situated within a spacious garden, with an extensive view towards the south. A piece of water near it greatly adds to the beauty of the scene.

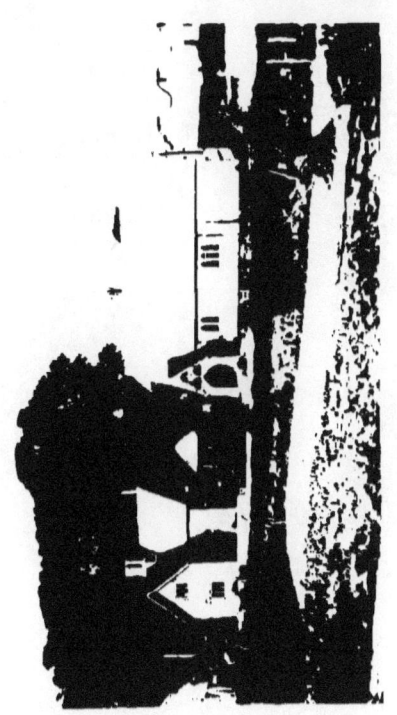

PITT.

No. 30.

FOR many years a service was held once a-week in a cottage at Pitt, which is an outlying hamlet of Hursley, about three miles distant from the parish church, and two from Winchester. By this arrangement many persons (especially the aged) were enabled to join in the church service who would otherwise have been deprived of it. Still the author of "The Christian Year" was hardly satisfied that God's service should be publicly celebrated in a poor cottage; and his wish for a worthier place in this little hamlet was gratified about the year 1858 by the liberality of the author of "The Heir of Redclyffe," who spent about £800 of the profits of her well-known talent, upon the erection of a school-chapel, designed by W. Butterfield, Esq. In this chapel a day-school is kept for the children of the hamlet, and public service is celebrated every Sunday by one of the Hursley clergy. There is also a residence for a schoolmaster, which was built soon after the chapel, by the joint exertions of several contributors.

BOURNEMOUTH.
No. 31.

HAVING now briefly alluded to the places with which Mr. KEBLE was chiefly connected during his lifetime, it is our sad task to direct the reader's mind to the house in which he died.

From October, 1865, till his death in March, 1866, he was entirely resident at Bournemouth. At first he had there an inconvenient lodging, but it was soon exchanged for Brookside, which will henceforth become famous as the great Christian Poet's last home on earth.

This cheerful house faces the south and east, looking towards the sea, of which it has an extensive view.

Bournemouth was just the place for the holy man. The church and its services were well accordant with his heavenly tastes; the daily prayer was a great comfort to him, the sea-shore a constant source of interest and delight.

We can fancy many an invalided clergyman, in years yet to come, going to Bournemouth to recruit his health, (or it may be to spend his last days on earth,) with eagerness asking which was the Poet's last home, and looking with deep reverence upon that house in which the spirit of the author of "The Christian Year" fled from its prison-house of earth.

We may trust that the memory of Mr. and Mrs. KEBLE—two saints who are gone—may be of use to some in that quiet watering-place, as a help in preparing for the rest which is without doubt their portion for ever.

THE GRAVES.
No. 32.

TWO little mounds of earth (at present simply but neatly covered with turf) in Hursley churchyard, mark the double grave of Mr. and Mrs. KEBLE. Their names are written in the hearts of the poor who loved them.

> "Far better they should sleep awhile
> Within the Church's shade,
> Nor wake, until new heaven, new earth,
> Meet for their new immortal birth
> For their abiding-place be made."
> *(Hymn for Burial of the Dead.)*

Some great building may, we trust, ere long be raised as a memorial to the loved name of KEBLE. At Hursley he has built his own memorial in the model church, and in the hearts of those to whom he ministered. Yea, his memorial is throughout the world: and he will reap eternally the fruit of all his labours.

> "Thus learn us, Lord, to count our days,
> Till we, with purpose strong,
> A wise heart offer to Thy praise:
> Return, O Lord—how long?"
> *(Psalm 90.)*

ERRATUM.

Page 23, last line but one, for "vigorously" read "rigorously."

W. SAVAGE will be happy to supply any of the Views in this Work, either separately or in small or large numbers, as "Cartes de Visite," where the print will admit of it, 1s. *each, or* 10s. 6d. *per dozen; the full print, mounted on board ten inches by eight,* 1s. 6d. *each, or* 15s. *per dozen. Postage extra. They can also be had unmounted, if required, for the Album or foreign postage.*

W. S. has photographed nearly the whole of Hursley, including the Schoolhouses, Lych-gate, and every interesting subject in the village and neighbourhood, all of which can be supplied as above.

Gentlemen's Estates photographed, and everything appertaining to the art executed at his Studio, 97, HIGH-STREET, WINCHESTER.

www.ingramcontent.com/pod-product-compliance
Lightning Source LLC
Chambersburg PA
CBHW030334170426
43202CB00010B/1119